MW00715624

To Love Again

Jean Monbourquette

To Love Again

Finding Comfort and Meaning in
Times of Grief

NOVALIS

Cover art, layout and design: Carroll Burritt

Illustrations: Muriel Faille

Photos: Gilles Guttadauria: 4, 36, 58, 85, 109, 130; Carroll Burritt: 16;
Gilles Savoie: 30; Paul Hamel: 92; Mia & Klaus: 103; Jos Kane: 104;
Anne McLaughlin: 125; Mary Kibblewhite: 126; W.V.D. Kallen: 138;
H. Armstrong Roberts: 156.

Translation: Brigitte Caron

© 1993 Novalis, Saint Paul University, Ottawa

Business Office: Novalis, 49 Front Street East, 2nd Floor, Toronto, Ontario M5E 1B3.
Editorial Office: Novalis, 223 Main Street, Ottawa, Ontario K1S 1C4.

Printed in Canada

Canadian Cataloguing in Publication Data

Monbourquette, Jean
      To love again: finding comfort and meaning in
times of grief

Translation of: Aimer, perdre et grandir
ISBN 2-89088-615-8

      1. Suffering — Psychological aspects.
2. Separation (Psychology).   3. Loss (Psychology).
4. Love.   5. Death.   I. Title.

BF789.S8M6513 1993   152.4   C93-090332-3

Acknowledgements

To the ones who confided in me, my teachers:

The following pages are the product of my own reading and personal experience. They arise from a desire to understand the personal tragedies of friends and clients who have confided in me.

I thank them for their trust and for allowing me to enter their wounded world.

Through hearing their secrets and witnessing their courage and their determination to heal and to grow, I have discovered a great deal about the mystery of suffering and about life itself.

To my readers:

I ask that you read this book through the knowing of the heart; it must be read as it was written. This book contains a very loose linking thread that may, at times, seem repetitive. I have tried to follow the movement of the heart and its unpredictable patterns. Some of you will read it from cover to cover, others will meditate on it, many will refer back to those passages that most inspire them.

This book is intended to accompany you on your journey inward. Some pages may upset you a little, some may upset you a great deal. If so it may be wiser to put off reading those passages when you are in a fragile state. I am thinking, for example, of those of you who feel deeply hurt and find the very idea of forgiving intolerable.

Many people have contributed their talent to this book. I would like to express my gratitude especially to Muriel Faille for the magic of her drawings and their hopeful message and to Carroll Burritt for graphic design and layout as well as for the cover design and artwork.

To Love Again is more than a mere translation of *Aimer, perdre et grandir* because I have added more than forty pages of new material and reorganized the presentation of the themes of grief according to a more natural healing process.

I want to express a very special thanks to Brigitte Caron and Carroll Burritt for their precise and elegant translation. I know that their main inspiration for doing this work stems from their desire to help people in the midst of their suffering. This is their way of offering comfort and meaning to those who are experiencing losses in their lives.

And thank you also to all the readers of previous French editions who have contributed to it in a thousand different ways.

Jean Monbourquette

Contents

Introduction	1
I do not want to lose my love	5
I am waiting	17
How long must I suffer	31
I go on living	59
I allow myself to heal	93
I am growing	127

*I*ntroduction

The pages of my own book

The pages that we wrote together,
I am still writing them alone,
in your absence,
in your silence,
to the rhythm of my own pain.

I continue writing my own story,
in the joy of healing,
in the need for forgiveness,
in the hope of renewal.

To you my friend

I am writing to you who are suffering from a deep loss in your life. I hope that reading these pages will bring you comfort; I want to be with you in the solitude of your pain that may sometimes feel like despair.

I want to sustain you with testimonies and suggestions. It is said that a "good" counsellor must avoid giving too much advice. I know by experience, however, that in difficult moments, a strong and warm presence can help me out of my lethargy.

In the same way the physical body heals a physical wound, the emotional body begins a healing process the moment the emotional trauma occurs. Allow the natural wisdom of your healing system to come to your rescue. Trust it, and it will tend your emotional wounds. Eventually the pain will subside, and you will then be more aware of life around you, more open to happiness, more human.

Throughout this journey that you are about to begin, I would like you to face your pain and to recognize it peacefully. This attitude will help you survive. It will facilitate your healing process and actually help you to benefit from your own suffering.

Jean Monbourquette

Chapter 1

 do not want to lose

my love

To lose

Fists clenched,
I was holding on to you,
my love.

Through my fingers,
like gold dust,
you slipped away.

What have you lost?

I invite you to embrace your human condition. You cannot avoid losing and suffering in order to grow. This is part of the cycle of life.

> *The bud opens to produce the flower.*
> *The flower wilts to produce new seeds.*
> *The seed withers to germinate.*
> *This is the continuous cycle of life and death,*
> *of darkness and light.*

Death makes no sense unless it yields new life.
I would like to draw up a list of potential losses with you.
Keep in mind, while reading this list, that every loss can be transformed into a gain, into an opportunity for personal growth.

Small losses and daily annoyances

A missed opportunity.
A toothache.
Bugs in your favourite house plant.
A cat that does not come home one night.
A missed date.
The short-term absence of a friend.

Shocking losses

Being robbed.
Losing a large sum of money.
Not getting an expected contract.
Being laid off without warning.
For an alcoholic, giving up the bottle.
Finding out that you have a serious illness.
Completing a project and feeling the letdown.
Moving from your nice neighbourhood.
Losing your good reputation unfairly.
Leaving a comfortable job, even for a promotion,
And so on.

Unavoidable human losses

Losing your childhood illusions.
Leaving home for the first time.
Losing your adolescent dreams.
Losing friendships from childhood to adulthood.
Not living up to your potential.
Losing your youth.
Reaching menopause (men and women).
Your last child leaving home.
Losing your attractiveness.
Losing your sexual potency when you still have the desire.
Losing your passion.
Losing your teeth, your hair, your sight.
Growing old.

The great losses in love

A friendship coming to an end.
The end of an intimate relationship.
A separation, a divorce.
The death of a loved one.

Losing in death, losing in life

Death does not take away a loved one in the same way life does. In both cases, there is a separation, a rupture, but you do not experience them in the same manner.

To be separated by death means a point of no return; it is final, the person is no longer accessible. When you are separated from someone who is still living, it is not as final. You can still see each other, and often, you must see each other. In this situation, recent scars can again become wounds.

When your spouse passes away, friends and objects may remind you of him or her, but when you are separated because of divorce, you must continue to deal with your ex-spouse. You must divide up property, consult each other about the children, the parents, the mutual friends. A recently divorced man said that he was tired of finishing business with his ex-wife. He felt as though he was trying "to cut off ties with a small, rusty knife."

Given the sense of failure surrounding a divorce, ex-spouses may end up quarrelling and misunderstanding each other even more, as if they were sinking in a swamp of misunderstanding. When loved ones are snatched by death, it is over. They become forever idealized. Only the happy moments and memories stand out, obscuring the sometimes painful moments that are inevitable in married life.

To leave or to be left?

There is a great difference between leaving somebody and being left by somebody.

If you are the one initiating the separation, you find yourself in an advantageous position. You have power, especially if you are planning to begin a new relationship.

On the other hand, the one who initiates a separation may feel guilty and dishonest. How can you leave someone gracefully, as it were? There are steps that you can take to separate with fairness.

1. Speak of your intention to separate if the relationship does not improve, thus avoiding a sudden and vengeful departure.

2. If, in time, you see no improvement, tell him or her with conviction that you want to separate.

3. Before splitting up, there is no need to burden your partner with blame, (as there is no need to accuse your dog of having rabies if you have to get rid of it).

4. If possible, help your spouse or friend to find resources that may cushion the blow of your departure.

5. Do not forget to go through your own grieving process before getting involved with someone else.

What about the person left behind?

If you have been left behind, especially if you have not seen it coming, you are usually the most affected by the separation. Therefore, you must find ways to gain control over the situation.

- Stop holding on to the other person.
- Decide to leave your mate.
- Do all that you can to bring this about.
- Avoid playing the role of the martyr.
- Take an active part in the separation process, even though you did not want it.

Possibly you will hurt more than your spouse; but I can assure you that, if you become an actor in your own drama, rather than a spectator, you will gain an unexpected maturity.

Remember that the one who initiates the separation may have often felt neglected. And it is not always clear who left whom first.

Life-giving emptiness

All the love.
All the talent.
All the time.
All the attention.
All the joy.
All the tenderness.
All the suffering.
All the promises.
All the caring.
All is lost!

There is only a void.
Only death.
Only nothingness.
There is grace in recognizing the obvious.
Hard and reassuring reality.
Total surrender.
My suffering is transformed into light,
into purification,
into bursting life.
Why must I die in order to learn how to live?

Stop tormenting your heart

After losing someone, many questions may well up within you:

"Why me?"

"Why now?"

"What have I done to deserve this?"

"Why is God testing me this way?"

And so on.

Be patient

"Be patient in the absence of answers," says the poet.
Stop harassing your heart and your spirit.
They are unable or unwilling to answer you.
They know that some of those answers may be unbearable
to you right now.
For the present, welcome these questions without trying to
find answers. Let yourself experience these questions.
One day you will find yourself living those very answers.

Chapter 2

 am waiting

The wait

Waiting in anguish, in doubt; uncertainty is a loss in itself. Life is standing still. You lose energy through wondering, speculating, expecting the worst. Uncertainty destroys your enjoyment of life.

"Is the tumour malignant?"
"Will I be healthy again?"
"Will our friendship be the same after our fight?"
"When will my spouse's infidelities stop?"
"Does she want a divorce?"
"Does he want to leave me?"
"Will I pass my exam?"
"Will I receive this promotion?"
"Will I get this job?"
"Is my financial decision sound?"

Not knowing is extremely painful; some prefer a negative outcome to the discomfort of waiting. Waiting is like losing; you lose your inner peace, your serenity, your joy of living.

Know that you can use this time of waiting constructively. You can spend time caring for yourself, you can still enjoy yourself, continue living and living well.

To be depressed, to feel paralysed and frightened serves no purpose. Get back in physical and psychological shape so you can face the outcome, positive or negative.

Drifting in the void

I am waiting and waiting.
I am waiting for an outcome that I want, that I fear.
A thousand times I have thought of ways to hold on to you.
A thousand times I felt that I was losing you.
I falter.
I am no longer the master of my emotions.
I feel angry about that.

I feel too vulnerable, too dependent on your decision.
In this state of continuous doubt, I waste time thinking and rethinking.
Where is my inner guide when my thoughts get tangled and contradictory?

The painful presence

When I was alone with myself,
I enjoyed my own company.
When I met you,
I felt even better.

When you are with me without being fully present,
I feel anxious.
I cannot live with only half of you.
Your presence only reminds me of what I am losing.

Ambivalence about grief

I want to be freed from my anxiety and pain, but I know that, first, I must deeply experience these feelings. This frightens me.

I feel that, before I am able to think of others, I must look after myself.

Though I know that I will never forget my lover, I have the right not to think of him all the time.

To regain my autonomy, I must become dependent and accept the help of others.

I need to live for today in the face of pain that pulls me towards the past.

I do not want to be alone, but I am afraid of being smothered by the pity of others.

I want to believe that some day, my beloved will be present for me in some mysterious way, but I am afraid to let go of the physical bonds that still bind us.

I believe that eventually I will heal and grow, but this "small death" that is my bereavement makes me tremble.

Love is not always blind

One day I was struck by these lines written on a poster:
"If you love him, set him free;
If he comes back it is because he has never forgotten you.
If he does not, forget him."

I thought about this poem and came up with my own version:
"If you love someone, do not let him go
without telling him of your pain, and the difficulties
that his decision will cause in your life."

If your beloved returns, do not accept him back before making sure that, during his absence, he has resolved his inner conflicts and has grown.

If your beloved has not returned, do not wait indefinitely; bid your dreams goodbye.

Life has much more in store for you.

Letting go of you

In the midst of my despair,
I sometimes get a sense of immense freedom
by simply letting go of you.
I stop waiting for
a letter,
a phone call,
a card that never comes.
I stop
the speculations,
the intimate conversations
that will not take place.

Since your departure
I have more time
for myself,
for my friends,
for the books that I always wanted to read.
I have less insomnia.
I have more happiness and more joy.
Letting go of you is simple, and yet,
just the thought of it
takes my breath away!

A hundred times, I wanted to stop my imagination

I am trying so desperately to control my mind
and my thoughts.
So often during the day I catch myself dreaming
that my lover comes back to me,
that my lover needs me,
that my lover misses me,
that my lover is unhappy with "the other,"
that my lover will return, asking for forgiveness,
that I will welcome my lover like "the prodigal child."

Then the dream vanishes and there is only the harsh
reality of her absence.
So I have decided to stop wrestling with my imagination.
From now on I will allow it total freedom.
I will be freer to write a different ending to the story, to
enjoy this fantasy,
and when sorrow overrides the fantasy
I will welcome it gently.

How long are you going to wait?

When the loss of love is obvious, you can start letting go right away.

Sometimes the separation is decided by the other person. You are waiting for him to ask you to marry, or you wonder if your spouse will come back home or ask for a divorce.

When the state of uncertainty is created by the other person, you must try to gain control over the situation, try to play an active role in making the decision.

Set a time limit – two weeks, three months, a year – as to how long you are willing to wait for a positive outcome. Make this deadline binding by telling the other person and by informing a few close friends.

In the meantime, continue to live for yourself and to live well. If, on the contrary, you fall into a passive and gloomy attitude, you will only become more depressed. Keep busy, enjoy yourself, be prepared for all possibilities. Get legal advice regarding your rights if you decide to put an end to a legal union. Find out about job opportunities, about returning to school, and so on.

When the deadline arrives, if nothing has changed, you must act by formally announcing that the relationship is over, and by starting the grieving process, this time for good.

If you do this, you will not be tossed around by uncertainty. You will be in control of your life, even through this difficult period. As you begin to grieve, you will set out on the road to healing. And believe me, you will heal.

Imminent losses; anticipated grief

You know that your friend will die, that the illness is incurable, that the separation is imminent.

You can make the grieving process easier by beginning to say goodbye right away.

- Tell the other person how you feel.
- If you are dying, take time to share with the ones you are leaving behind.
- Share your emotions, your needs, your decisions.
- Tell them your hopes for the future.
- Grant forgiveness and ask for forgiveness.

If another person is not ready to grant forgiveness, or to accept yours, you can express it in the quiet of your heart while in the presence of this person. You will be amazed at the liberating power of this silent dialogue.

Last words

I know someone very important who prepared his departure thoroughly.

"Now I am going to the one who sent me.
It is for your own good that I am going
because unless I go,
my Spirit will not come to you
but if I go, I will send him to you.

"In a short while you will no longer see me,
and then a short time later you will see me again.
I tell you most solemnly, you will be weeping and wailing
but your sorrow will turn to joy.

"I shall see you again and your hearts will be full of joy,
and that joy no one shall take from you."

Saint John

I fear the holidays

I fear the holidays and the anniversaries:
Mother's Day, Father's Day,
her birthday,
our wedding anniversary,
the date of his departure, of his death,
Christmas, New Year's Day,
all the other holidays and anniversaries.

I am afraid to awaken my sleeping sorrow.
I am afraid of the happy memories that only
make my pain stand out more.
I stay away from happy people,
especially those who want to entertain me.
My soul is drifting and I feel sad.
I want to hide.

Chapter 3

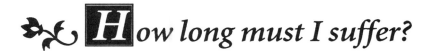 *ow long must I suffer?*

How much time should you spend grieving?

This is a question to which there is not just one correct answer. The duration of the grieving process will depend on each person and on a host of factors. I will list these factors as questions to help you identify your specific situation.

Whom have you lost? A parent, a spouse, a child, a friend...?
(It seems to me that the death of a child would be the most painful, and would require the longest grieving period.)
How did the separation come about? A long illness, an accident, a suicide, an unexpected divorce, a betrayal, an unfaithfulness, a negotiated separation...?
Was there time to prepare for the separation before it happened? If so, how did you prepare for it?
How did you experience grieving in your own family?

How would you describe your relationship when the person died, or when the separation occurred (frustrating, depressing, happy)?
What other losses, or concerns, did you have at the time of the separation?
Do you have free time to allow yourself to begin the grieving process?

What support do you have to help you go through these difficult moments? Friends, relatives, professionals, a community, a support group...?

Some say that one never really gets over grieving. However, there is no doubt that pain diminishes with time. In traditional societies, it is believed that it takes nine months – the duration of a pregnancy. I believe that getting over the grief caused by separation from a loved one takes at least two years.

The amount of time devoted to grieving is very important, but what is even more crucial is what we actually do, and the decisions we make during that time.

The stages of grieving

Only recently have grief counsellors started to explore the various stages of grief. Traditional civilizations have been aware of this process for a long time. These civilizations practised rituals that helped them overcome a separation or an emotional loss. In our modern societies we need to rediscover ways of dealing with the pain of grief, of healing ourselves and of growing through this experience.

Professional counsellors suggest various methods of getting over grief. As a result of my experience and my studies, there are a number of reference points that I use to help people experience grief and grow from it. Each reference point corresponds to a different stage:

First stage: shock

Second stage: denial

Third stage: expressing emotions and feelings

Fourth stage: completing the tasks related to grieving

Fifth stage: discovering the meaning of the loss

Sixth stage: forgiveness

Seventh stage: claiming the legacy

Eighth stage: celebrating the end of grief.

Joys and losses, the fabric of daily life

Whether our loss is great or small we go through the same stages. Only the duration and the intensity of the emotions vary in relation to the degree of emptiness that follows the loss of a loved one. In the case of a spouse, or someone very close, it can take two or three years before we feel whole again. On the other hand, the feeling of loss can disappear after a few minutes if the relationship is superficial.

Take, for example, a missed rendezvous with an old friend at the train station. You get there and the train is leaving. Here is a possible emotional scenario:

Shock and denial:	"I cannot believe I missed her."
Emotional outburst:	"I should have left work earlier." "Why did I get stuck in traffic. If only the traffic cops did their job properly."
Completing the task:	"I can phone her to explain what happened, and visit her later."
Discovering the significance:	"I will learn to plan ahead so that I will be punctual."
Forgiveness	"It's not the end of the world. I can forgive myself."

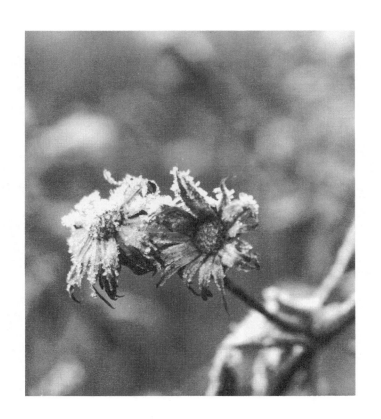

First stage: shock

When there is a surge of power that would cause electrical wires to burn, the fuses give out to prevent damage. When the suffering is too great, the human body produces tranquilizing hormones, nervous connections fail, reality becomes blurry and emotions stagnate.

These survival mechanisms are activated in times of great distress. They allow the victim of a tragedy to go on living, without falling apart, and to find resources to assist in confronting this harsh reality.

Here are the signs of a person in a state of shock:
- apparent insensitivity to a tragedy;
- buzzing in the ears, to avoid hearing bad news;
- blurred vision, so as not to see;
- a sensation of cold, and inner paralysis;
- physical heaviness, upon learning of a loved one's death;
- uncontrollable laughter in the face of a tragedy;
- hallucinations about the return of the person who has left.

If the state of shock lasts too long, it may affect the person's vitality. It may cause emotional numbness, dulling of pleasant, as well as painful, emotions and stiffening of the body. Consequently, this state of shock brings on a loss of energy, in addition to the loss that caused the grief.

Second stage: denial

A state of shock can cause, to varying degrees, a denial of reality. Your mind may play tricks on you, and you may find yourself thinking:

"It is not true."

"This is a dream."

"I just cannot believe it."

"I saw him only yesterday."

"She is not gone, she is still living."

"I have not touched his things yet; it is as though he were still here."

"I feel her presence in my prayers."

The people who surround you, often, encourage you to deny reality:

"Why talk about it? It will only make you sad."

"Do not cry. Forget it. Try to keep busy!"

"Why worry about it?"

Refusing to experience pain can be very destructive in itself. It can cause a stifling, agitating feeling of uneasiness. The body tries to protect itself by building a shell and soon becomes accustomed to it. Awareness becomes dulled, and the armour, which is supposed to protect and save life, begins to stifle it.

How can you differentiate between the paralysing pain of denial, and the sharp pain of realizing your great loss? The pain of loss is sudden, burning and intense, but thank God it does not last. It also makes room for other emotions, heralding the rebirth of life.

Forms of denial

Denial takes on many different forms:
- ☐ forgetting the anniversary of death;
- ☐ performing the cremation quickly without a proper farewell ceremony;
- ☐ avoiding anything connected with dying and death, such as: hospitals, cemeteries, doctors, priests;
- ☐ keeping busy in order to avoid grieving;
- ☐ trying to find someone to blame for the death or the breakup;
- ☐ keeping the memory of the departed person alive with photographs and mementos;
- ☐ clinging to the departed by preserving their things, and the place where they lived;
- ☐ abusing medication, alcohol, drugs.

However, the most damaging form of denial is trying to imitate, or to replace, the person who is gone, to avoid grieving.

- ☐ The oldest son feels the need to take the place of the deceased father.
- ☐ A child starts imitating the behaviour of her deceased sibling.
- ☐ The son tries to become the husband after the father has left.
- ☐ The newly divorced man remarries immediately, in the hope of finding comfort and consolation.

In all these cases, trying to replace the family member who has left or died instead of going through your own grief is very harmful.

The heart that refuses to suffer

During a group session, Helena, a nun, told the group that she had just left a priest whom she loves very much. The separation occurred willingly and rationally. She decided to give him up to protect her vocation.

She talked about her love affair as if it were a trivial event, and she claimed that she was very comfortable with her decision. These last words made me uneasy. So I asked her about the pain that she must have experienced. She answered that it was all behind her. Then, the next day, she came to see me and told about a dream that she had had the night before.

"I was sitting on my bed and my left breast was swelling out of proportion; I was holding it in my hands trying to stop it from growing. All of a sudden a large wound appeared at the base of my breast and released grey and dried tissues. Then I woke up feeling surprised and sad that dead skin was coming out of this wound."

I asked her to go back to the dream and to imagine that blood was coming out of the wound. She responded matter-of-factly that there was no blood. I encouraged her to try to imagine drops of blood coming out of the wound.

At that moment Helena's tense face began to relax, and tears started to roll down her cheeks. She nodded to let me know that she was now seeing blood coming out of the wound.

Her repressed pain was surfacing and she was willing to accept and experience it.

She was no longer afraid. She was hurting, but she was also alive.

Third stage: expressing emotions and feelings

This is an important stage in the grieving process. It allows the human psyche to free itself from the biological and psychological bonds linking it to the lost person. This is not the final stage, as many would believe.

However, it is a very dramatic one because it occurs immediately after the state of shock, and the stage of denial, when close friends and relatives begin to leave the grieving person alone. They assume that the person is now strong enough to deal with the loss on his own.

At this stage, you will become increasingly aware of many emotions: fear, powerlessness, sadness, guilt, anger, perhaps even a feeling of liberation. Only when you become fully aware of your loss and its implications will you have completed this stage. Many grieving people are unable to reach this stage, let alone complete it. Why is this?

Because they cannot let themselves go.

Because they do not want to experience the feeling that they are regressing, and becoming like a child again.

Because they have never learned how to feel, and express, certain emotions.

Because they are afraid of expressing conflicting emotions towards the loved one, such as love and anger, for fear of being judged by friends and family.

Because they have a limited range of "acceptable" emotions.

Depression and guilt

Losing a loved one often attracts an insensitive, arrogant and accusing inner judge. The person who is experiencing pain may, at the same time, be blaming herself:

"I asked for it."
"I should have known that ..."
"I was stupid to think that ..."
"If I had not acted the way I did ..."

Guilt often feeds on a partner's last accusing words, spoken at the time of separation:

"You are no longer interesting."
"No matter what you do, it is hopeless."
"You are mean and dishonest."

This sort of dialogue causes painful emotions like depression, exhaustion and despair.

You may feel a strong tendency to compare yourself to others.

"This only happens to me."
"I will never be as lovable as ..."

You may feel physically exhausted (another reason to blame yourself). Sometimes you experience nervous chills throughout your body. Take this condition seriously. You should treat depression just like any other physical illness.

Anger

Some people tend to accuse others, which is often psychologically healthier, because it brings about momentary relief.

The ambulance did not get here fast enough ...
The priest did not know what to say ...
The doctor did not prescribe the right drug ...
He should have understood that ...

At other times, you ask yourself many questions. (You are less interested in getting answers than finding a culprit.)

Why me?
Why did you go?
Why did you leave me?
Why did God allow this to happen to me?
Why, why...?

Like a cry of rebellion, we are more interested in accusing someone than in finding out who the real culprit is.

Sometimes we curse the ones whom we blame for our unhappiness.

If only he were the one who had gotten sick!
Maybe she will have an accident!
One day, he will pay for what he did to me!
I do not believe in God anymore!

The full realization of the loss; the great lament

It is only gradually that you become aware of what you have lost.

You go through several minor passions before you enter the Great Passion that leads to renewed Life.

Your relatives and friends try to cushion the blow: "It will pass." "You are getting better." "You will forget her." "You have to go on living." They try encouraging you to become rational.

Then suddenly, one day, something happens; a dramatic incident, a chance meeting, and in a flash it all becomes clear: "It is over. I have loved and now my beloved is gone forever."

Slowly, sadness overtakes your entire being, every fibre of your body and soul. You fall into the abyss that you have been avoiding for so long. You lose track of time and place. You sob uncontrollably, your body is shaken by the convulsions of sorrow. You worry that you are losing your mind.

And then, when you are not even expecting it, you see a glimpse of light at the end of the tunnel. You begin to enter a new world. You are uplifted with a feeling of liberation. You have survived the storm and lived to see a bright and peaceful day.

The emotional merry-go-round

It would be very simple if you could follow the sequence of emotions described above. Unfortunately, emotions and feelings have a way of defying clear categories.

More often than not you will be assailed by unexpected feelings such as fear, anger, guilt, shame or sadness. You may even feel liberated from the person you love.

Try to let yourself experience these feelings as much as you can. It is often easier to do so with a person you trust.

By nature, emotions are transitory and temporary. If you find that you are clinging to one in particular, it may be that an underlying emotion is not able to surface.

A lasting feeling of anger is often the result of a deeply repressed psychological wound.

A permanent attitude of sadness may feed on an unconscious rage.

A strong desire for isolation (compulsive independence) may be caused by a frustrated need for dependence.

An uncontrollable fear may stem from an undercurrent of pain and rebellion.

Feelings of guilt and shame often result from self-hatred and anger.

Let the river of your emotions run its course; it will lead you to the peaceful waters of inner tranquility.

Fourth stage: completing the tasks related to grieving

Once you have experienced some emotional catharsis, it is important to move on to accomplishing tasks that will reflect the inner detachment that you have achieved.

It is time to:
- ☐ attend to unfinished business through writing and other farewell rituals;
- ☐ complete funeral arrangements such as burying the ashes, choosing a tomb stone, and so on;
- ☐ keep any promise made at the time of separation.

(If it is impossible to keep a particular promise, find another way to keep your word. For example, if you promised your wife that you would never remarry after she passes away and then you meet someone that you love very much, and wish to marry, replace that promise by another one such as bringing flowers to your deceased wife's grave every month for six months.

Make this new promise binding by telling someone important such as a priest, a lawyer or a parent. This ritual will help to bring a sense of completion to your relationship with your spouse.)

When ready, remove the photographs and put them in an album; sell, or give away, the belongings of the loved one.

These tasks may seem unimportant, but performing them will speed up your grieving process.

Fifth stage: discovering the meaning of the loss

Psychiatrist Victor Frankl suggests that to regain your zest for life you must satisfy a very basic human need by finding meaning in what has happened to you. You can begin doing this as soon as you are off the initial emotional roller-coaster and have gained some sense of perspective. You may need some help with this exercise, because the meaning may not be easy to discover at first.

Here are some questions that a friend can ask you to help you discover the meaning of your experience.
What impact will this separation have on your life?
How will this loss help you know yourself better?
What new resources have you found in yourself?
What lesson is this difficult situation teaching you?
Which way will your life go from here?
To what extent have you strengthened your faith?
How do you intend to grow from this painful experience?

These questions will cause you to reflect on the meaning of your experience. Trust your inner wisdom to find appropriate answers. You may find answers right away. At other times, you may be able to organize scattered thoughts into more precise answers. Or you may find yourself living the answers, without being aware of them.

Examples of people who found meaning in their tragedy

A divorced man: "It was only when my marriage failed that I realized how emotionally dependent on, and demanding of, my ex-wife I had been. Now, with the help of a psychologist, I am learning to become more autonomous."

A woman who lost her child at birth: "I know now that I did not lose my child in vain. I gave it up for adoption to my best friend who died regretting never having had children. Now my child has a mother in heaven, and my friend can take care of "her child."

A professor, as a result of a heartbreak: "I set up an association for people who feel they have experienced failure in their marriage or relationship. Before my own break-up, I would have never become involved with people this way."

A palliative caregiver: "After my fetus died I felt the need to assist people who were dying. This death in my life prepared me for my new mission. Now, I help the dying be born to eternal life."

A mother who lost her 19-year-old son in an accident: "I understood the message that my son had recorded for me on my birthday. It said: 'Thank you for being so forgiving.' These words inspired me to work with young adults because I felt that my role on earth was 'for giving'."

Sixth stage: forgiveness

Asking forgiveness

A major loss can be very self-revealing. For instance, you may suddenly realize how much you truly loved the person that you lost and how poorly you have expressed that love. To alleviate your feelings of guilt, you need to feel forgiven, and to forgive yourself.

But for what should you be forgiven?
For not living up to the expectations that you created in the other person?
For not having said often enough: "I love you"?
For having taken the other person for granted?
For not being able to save them from illness and death?
For not being able to save your marriage?
For lacking love and foresight?

Asking for forgiveness, even in the other person's absence, can alleviate your feelings of guilt. Once you feel forgiven you can start accepting yourself with your limitations, your faults, your shortcomings, etc. You are then ready to embrace peace within yourself.

Granting forgiveness

Once you start experiencing the peace that comes with feeling forgiven, you will be better prepared to forgive the person who left you. Obviously, in the case of death, forgiveness does not have the same intensity as in the case of divorce. In both cases, however, it is necessary to forgive in order to relieve, and even eliminate, the feelings of anger that separation has caused you.

Without forgiveness it is very difficult to move on to the next stage: claiming your legacy. How could you possibly accept an emotional legacy from someone with whom you are still angry?

Some people say that forgiving someone for dying is unnecessary because a person is not responsible for his death. On the other hand, they can understand why forgiving an ex-spouse is important. I say that forgiveness is important even when the separation is caused by death.

A relationship is never perfect, and intimate partners always have something to forgive of each other. In addition, you may resent your dead spouse for having abandoned you with the responsibility for the children's education, the bills, and your feelings of aloneness and pain.

By forgiving the other person you help to eliminate the feelings of resentment that you still carry.

Seventh stage: claiming the legacy

This stage is more than merely accepting the loss of a loved one and healing your wounds; it is even more than the return to a "normal" life. It is a way to lay claim to the very energy, love and qualities of the person that you have loved, and lost.

In any love relationship lovers often tend to create an ideal image of the beloved. It is even said that before being in love with a real person, men and women fall in love with an idealized lover. This phenomenon, made up of equal parts of fantasy and reality, accounts for the intensity of first loves. Infatuated lovers tell each other that it is as if they had always known each other.

When a separation occurs, former lovers feel that they are losing parts of themselves. In some cases, when a couple has been together for a long time and one of them dies, the other soon follows.

This is why, if you can reach this stage of healing and lay claim to the strengths and attributes of your beloved, you will enrich your own personality.

But, to inherit these qualities, you need to let go of your attachment to the other person.

(For the ritual of legacy, see pages 154 and 155.)

Eighth stage: celebrating the end of grief

How do you know that your grieving is over? In the old days, people announced the end of their mourning period by changing the colour of their clothing. Nowadays there are no such visible signs or social conventions to signal the end of the grieving period, so there is no way of knowing.

In grief support groups, after the ritual of the legacy has taken place, the leader officially declares that your grieving process is finished, in order to do away with this uncertainty.

Upon hearing this public announcement, those who have been grieving become filled with joy. They feel liberated. They experience a peace and inner harmony that washes away anguish, pain and depression. Some people even shed tears of joy.

I recommend that this celebration end with a prayer of thanksgiving, with congratulations and with a toast to new life.

Be patient with yourself

In this world, dominated by fast-food and the "throw-away" culture, I know that you would like to be able just to get rid of your pain. Unfortunately, it probably will not happen as fast as you would like.

The healing process must run its course. You can facilitate this process, but you cannot hurry it. Be careful not to skip any stages. The deeper your emotional wound, the longer the healing will take.

Be certain that healing will come. In fact, the healing process has already started within you. Give yourself as much time as you need, just as if you were letting a fractured limb mend itself. You deserve this time.

This human experience is important. You must live it well. Very few people take the time to become humanized by their suffering. They prefer either to harden their hearts or to try to forget. These latter options will make them very wary of loving again.

Suffering is not good in itself. Do not cultivate it for its own sake. But if you try to learn from it, you will reap enormous benefits in terms of maturity and personal growth.

Chapter 4

 I *go on living*

I am drowning

Wednesday: *I am becoming aware of his departure.*

Thursday: *I am drowning in my memories and I weep.*

Friday: *I am sinking into a dark depression.*

Saturday: *I feel like I am drowning.*

Sunday: *My God, I cannot come up to the surface. Do you make house calls?*

Fear of going crazy with sadness

Often people who go through difficult experiences fear that they will lose their minds.

This may be something that worries you also. Sometimes you may say to yourself:

"I have a difficult time getting a handle on myself."
"I will not be able to get better."
"I feel that I will have a nervous breakdown."
"I have lost everything; I do not know where I am going."
"I will not be able to hold on."

Your fear is real, but the object of your fear, namely "going crazy," may not be. I doubt that you will go as far as "losing your marbles."

Your present state is, to say the least, uncomfortable. You feel upset. You have lost you inner stability, and you are afraid.

Wisdom requires that you give yourself time. You should allow yourself to float without trying to resist it too much.

Already, inside you, new energy is building up, working towards a new sense of inner balance.

When I stopped being a couple

On the way home I stifled my desire to be with you.
I stopped pondering the events that I wanted to share
with you.
I missed your playful touch.
I held inside the long conversations I wanted to have
with you.
I could no longer ask you to hold me when I had
nightmares.

I no longer felt unconditionally accepted.
I destroyed the tape recording of our shared dreams.
I tried to stop worrying about your personal problems.
I tried to stop myself from being happy for you.
I have given up my role as your protector and confidant.
I have tried to bury a past that is still alive.
A great part of me has stopped living.

My freedom will come from what I fear most

My eyes are blurry.
My body is cold and tense.
My ears are ringing.
My thoughts are muddled.

This state of unconsciousness frightens me more than the loss of you.
How can I get over this?
I am afraid that the only way out is to welcome this unexpected guest called pain.

You belong to the community of the suffering

The very idea of being the only one suffering, among seemingly happy people, is often unbearable.

But you should know that right now, there are many others, who, like you, feel only half alive, burdened by pain, misery and suffering.

You may find the sight of happy people unbearable. But you will also notice those who are going through upheavals and serious difficulties. You probably know someone in your immediate circle who is in pain or grieving.

What you are experiencing is important. You must focus on your suffering to transform it, as soon as possible, into a positive experience.

You are an alchemist who is transforming a mere metal into precious gold through the process of grieving.

You are not alone. Join the community of the suffering. You are supported by many people who are sharing in this common human experience, and they sympathize with you.

I thought I was invincible

I built a fortress around my heart.
I dulled my body.
I was cut off from my emotions.
At times, this power over myself was exhilarating.
I was the master of my own destiny,
master of my suffering,
master of my unhappiness.
I was a kind of inaccessible hero,
an insensitive god.
My head ruled my life.
In this unreal atmosphere, I was free.

Then one day, my ivory tower came crashing down,
my strength caved in,
my convictions were shaken.
I was overcome by vertigo.
I felt afraid.
I felt needy.
I felt small.
I cried and shivered.
Farewell nobility, farewell greatness and divinity;
I had become myself.

You retain your wealth of resources

As a result of separation from a loved one, through divorce or death, you may lose your self-confidence, your ability to overcome this trial. Do you have this sense of desperation? Has your self-esteem suffered a serious blow? Are you hearing inner voices saying that you should have seen this coming, that you should have listened to people's advice, that you should have been more careful.

In these times of self-accusation, remembering that you never cease being a healthy and whole person, and that you possess all the resources necessary to heal and grow, is important.

Be aware of your inner voices. Instead of saying to yourself, "I am wounded," say: "I have suffered an emotional blow and I have the ability to heal." Instead of saying, "I am a failure," say: "I have had a failure and it can be fixed." In spite of your loss you remain a healthy and resourceful person.

Trust yourself. Trust your inner wisdom. It will help you to come out of this experience enriched.

Give yourself the right to suffer

Being unhappy in today's society is not popular. In fact, judging by the ads on television, happiness is very easy to find.

We want to be happy regardless of the costs. This is why we put our elders in institutions and our sick in hospitals, and why we ask undertakers to make our deceased look good.

We abhor suffering and fear. We are ashamed of our pain, and our sadness.

Give yourself permission to mourn, to weep and to be depressed for a while, even if, as a child, your parents forbid you to cry or to be be sad. Share with people who are wise, people who can accept your situation because they have been through it and know what you are experiencing.

This state is temporary. And with support and encouragement to express yourself you will begin to feel better.

I do not want to stop being the most important person in your life

I was never the best at anything.
For you, I was the most important,
the indispensable one,
the only one.

You told me that I was
the only one who understood you,
the only one who could reach you,
the only one who could console you,
the only one who could love you.

I cannot accept being just "a friend."
I cannot accept being like everyone else.
I cannot accept being just myself, without your admiration.
I want to be unique, unique in your eyes.

No more inner peace

Do not minimize the gravity of your loss!

You have been clobbered; your plans have been overturned, your inner peace has been shattered.

There is an insane dialogue going on in your head. The different voices are accusing each other; acting as if the leader of the group, or the conductor of the orchestra, has lost all control.

Some voices are accusing, others are apologizing:

"You should have acted differently."
"Yes, but I had no way of knowing."
"Forget him, he does not deserve you."
"Yes, but I am crazy about him."

This "multilogue" can become very tiresome and depressing. When you can, try to take charge and command all the conflicting voices to keep quiet, to give you a "break" and to be silent.

During this time of inner quietude, let your muscles and your nerves relax.

Open the dialogue with your inner child

You have felt how the various parts of yourself can be at odds with one another.

If you cannot talk with someone who will understand you, you can learn to console yourself. In the privacy of your room take a pillow in your arms and rock back and forth like children do.

Listen to your inner child.

Give this child a chance to speak, to cry, to weep.

Tell him that you understand his pain.
Remind her that you do not blame her
Let him know that you are there for him.
Assure her that you will not accuse her.

You may have to engage in this dialogue with your inner child many times before he relaxes and begins to open up.

Once you have established a relationship of trust with yourself, you will develop strength and inner peace.

You will become more present to yourself and compassionate with yourself.

Love and friendship litanies

I invite you to perform an exercise that can bring immediate relief when you are dealing with an inner monologue that is repetitive and depressing. I must admit that I do not believe in "gimmicks" but this exercise really works for me. Try it.

First of all, remember there is no need to attack the angry or depressing voice inside you. It is more helpful to use this repetitiveness to your advantage.

To perform this exercise effectively you should first make yourself comfortable, relax and start reciting the names of people, pets, even plants and objects that love you.

> *Cathy loves me.*
> *Tim loves me.*
> *My mother loves me.*
> *My cat loves me.*
> *Christine loves me.*
> *My hibiscus loves me.*

Keep reciting this litany without making any judgment on the nature, the quality or the intensity of their love for you. The important thing is to know that you are loved. Add to this list and repeat it over and over. In a few minutes you will become aware of a wonderful change within yourself.

The ups and downs of the healing process

You have set out on the road to healing!
This process does not take place progressively.

Healing is a winding road with many unexpected variations:
sudden highs, discouraging set backs, reassuring plateaus.

If you feel a regression, do not be discouraged. A new high is
sure to follow.

Little by little you will notice that the setbacks are not as
drastic or as frequent as they once were.

Already, anxiety is loosening its grip. The knot in your
stomach eases. There is less tension in your neck. You can
breathe more easily.

You feel better now!

My beloved, I could not see your flaws

Somedays I think that I will never be happy again.
I will never love again.
I will never be at peace again.
I feel that when I lost you I lost everything.
The "soul of my soul" ceased to exist.

And I forget how angry I felt with you sometimes,
how bored I was with you,
how I wanted to be somewhere else,
how I felt a prisoner of our relationship (O sweet prison!).

When I recall our conflicts,
our confrontations,
our unhappiness and our mutual frustration,
I feel better.
And I feel like going on living.

The importance of eating well

Eating well will accelerate your healing process.

Eat balanced meals at regular intervals. This will give you another opportunity to reinforce your ability to lead a healthy life in spite of your pain.

Avoid severe diets; they often mask a desire for self-punishment.

You may want to consult a nutritionist and ask her to prescribe a diet that will promote fitness and health.

Although there are no miracle products or recipes, there are foods, vitamins (for example, a combination of vitamins B and C), and herb teas that have calming and comforting effects on the body. You have everything to gain from finding out how these can help you.

This grieving process, to which you are devoting generous time, is stressful enough without making it more painful through a poor diet.

The dangers of numbing yourself

There is a big difference between seeking comfort from a friend to alleviate your pain and seeking comfort from artificial substances.

You should stay away from substances that prevent you from experiencing your emotions. They only foster emotional denial and delay your healing process.

Indulgences such as drinking alcohol, taking drugs, eating too many sweets, drinking coffee excessively or smoking too much may provide temporary relief, but they will cause harmful side effects such as loss of energy and even depression.

What about medication prescribed by a physician? It is recommended to take medication as prescribed. It may be like a crutch which will help you go on walking for a while.

However, only you know what you are feeling. Therefore, after consulting your doctor, you can decide to cut down on the dosage and notice how you feel. This way you will be better equipped to know when to quit medication altogether.

A personal first aid kit

Here are a few suggestions to help you "pamper" yourself during difficult times. They make hardships easier to bear.

- ☐ Take a warm bath with soothing oils.
- ☐ Go for a walk in nature.
- ☐ Have a massage.
- ☐ Take time to meditate and pray.
- ☐ Get ready for sleep by first winding down in the evening.
- ☐ Go to a movie or try out a new restaurant.
- ☐ Volunteer your time to help a friend or a community organization.
- ☐ Make an appointment with the hairdresser and be pampered for a while.
- ☐ Visit someone who is sick.
- ☐ Cook your favourite dish.
- ☐ Listen to your favourite music.
- ☐ Listen to a relaxation tape.
- ☐ Play with a child.
- ☐ Play with your pet.

These are inexpensive activities that can be very comforting. The important thing is to treat yourself with respect; to avoid punishing yourself as if you deserved what has happened to you.

Assess your level of energy

Grieving requires a lot of physical and mental energy. So when you feel tired, be generous with yourself and rest right away.

Sleep longer than usual; go to bed earlier and get up later.

Though temporary, grieving causes a constant stress.

Since your capacity to concentrate is diminished you should plan your activities carefully.

Postpone important decisions.

Avoid situations and people that require too strong an emotional commitment or that simply take too much energy.

Take on tasks and activities that you find relaxing and restful. This is no time to initiate important changes in your life.

If you have to deal with a stressful situation, ask for help. Avoid risky situations such as dangerous sports or fast driving.

Think of how you have overcome situations just as painful in the past.

Keep to your daily routine

There may be mornings when you will not feel like going to work. Get out of bed and start your day. There may be evenings when you feel like sitting in front of a noisy television and dwelling on somber thoughts.

Instead of surrendering to these moods, find constructive and relaxing activities. Give yourself moments of retreat during the day. A man told me that when he was in his office he could rarely find time to be alone, in peace, so the washroom became his oasis for regrouping.

Even though your heart is in turmoil, keep to your daily routine. Following a regular schedule will give you the feeling that you are leading a normal and structured life.

When you catch yourself having a useless argument with yourself over the simplest tasks, such as what to eat or what to wear, put a stop to it. Perform these daily tasks mechanically.

Instead of letting grief take over your entire day, set aside specific times when you can express your emotions more freely.

Make as few decisions as possible

Do not plan to make important decisions for the time being, unless it is absolutely necessary.

If you must make a decision, ask a wise and trusted friend or relative to help you. Even though your loved one has passed away, you can ask them to assist you.

"What would you do if you were me?"

Listen to the response in your heart.

This hardship may have affected your judgement. But the separation may also have given you the inner freedom to deal with your situation.

For now you have enough changes in your life. The wisest decision may be not to make any, if there is no pressing need.

I do not want to spend autumn alone

Autumn is upon me.
The cold chills me.
The trees are falling into slumber,
shedding their leaves.
The listlessness and nostalgia of
an imminent burial
arise within me.

Like the dying man
who refuses to die before
someone has cradled him,
I try not to die to my lover before
someone has said "I love you."
I do not want to spend autumn alone.

You have the right to be a child again

You have the right to regress, to become childlike for a while. It is essential that you do so to express your emotions and thus regain your balance.

Trust that this return to childhood is only temporary. The adult in you will soon take control of your situation again.

You have the right to seek comfort and understanding from a close relative or friend. You may need a hug. Know that it is perfectly natural to ask for such gestures of affection from people who can give it to you spontaneously.

If you have difficulty making such requests or even reading these lines, I can understand. Making yourself dependent and vulnerable like this is threatening. Know that you can express this need while retaining full autonomy and self-control.

The forsaken friend

My friend,
I have forgotten you,
I have neglected you,
I have stopped seeing you
because of a love that no longer exists.

On my lonely journey,
I would like to send you a card,
an S.O.S., a cry.

In my heart, I am sure that you will welcome me,
in the name of our unforgotten friendship
built through our youth,
through our mutual dependence,
through aspiring to the same goal.

I need to know, to feel that you are listening to me.
Tell me.
Will you be there for me?

Do not hesitate to ask for help

Often we are ashamed of having been rejected and we choose to isolate ourselves. We are afraid of boring people with our problems. Instead of being vulnerable we choose to wear the super hero's mask.

Indeed, when we are in need, we are mostly afraid of letting our weak side show. We are afraid to ask for support.

Yet asking for help is the most human and courageous thing you can do. This is why people who are grieving have a support network made up of friends. It is often easier to call on friends, who have more distance and perspective, than on relatives, who are themselves grieving.

You can also join a support group of people who are going through a similar experience.

If you wish to remain anonymous, you can call a help line.

You can arrange to visit a friend, get invited for a meal, plan activities for the weekend.

You may find that a lot of people around you have the ability to listen and to be compassionate: the convenience store owner, a neighbour, the janitor... Be attentive and you may meet many wise angels!

Cultivate life around you

A palliative care worker told me that her work with dying people caused her to surround herself with living things and made her more attentive to the birth of life around her.

In your own way you are also experiencing a form of death in yourself. For that reason creating life around you is important.

Grow a garden.
Care for some plants.
Make an arrangement of wild flowers.
Walk in nature.
Hug a tree.
Watch the river flow.
Smile at a child.
Listen to the voice of your favourite singer.
Play with a pet.

Unlikely sources of support

At daybreak my desire for life was gone.
On my breakfast table,
I see my plant,
fragile being,
faithful and quiet presence.

On its leaves and delicate flowers,
I place my inner weariness
and pain.
And, suddenly,
I find the courage to go on.

Renew your faith

You need to find reference points within yourself.
Go back to your beliefs.
Read the books that taught you lessons –
that once inspired you.
Repeat the prayers that you used
to find consoling and reassuring
before falling asleep

Visit a chapel, a religious and
peaceful place.
If you are a believer, be sure to
ask God to help you find meaning
in what you are experiencing.

The sight of other people's happiness pains me

Somedays, I find other people's happiness intolerable.
I cannot stand happy families,
couples walking hand in hand,
friends laughing together, lovers kissing,
people enjoying each other's company.
I feel like an orphan, cheated by life.

I feel like rebelling or like drowning in my sorrows.
Other people's happiness is like vinegar on my open
wound.

I lose face, I am ashamed, I want to be alone. My fear of happy people is turning on me.

It becomes intolerable when I imagine that the person who left me is happy. Who can save me from this inner turmoil?

(Be aware that this happiness that you think you see in other people may be just a figment of your own imagination.)

Is vengeance a solution?

Your natural instinct in the face of this affront may be to retaliate, to hurt back, to try destroy the other person's happiness.

Vengeance will undoubtedly bring you immediate satisfaction, but it will be short lived. Moreover it may cause painful consequences. It may provoke a counterattack by your ex-partner and set you both on a vendetta that may result in many injuries without accomplishing anything.

This vengeful streak comes from the part of you that wants to re-establish your personal dignity. However, by attacking the other person, you will not regain your dignity. In fact you may end up hurting yourself even more deeply.

Vengeance is a winding road that leads nowhere. It is often a lame attempt to revive a dead relationship. It is a waste of time.

Once the legal matters are settled, you should limit your contacts with the other person to a minimum. You should start tending your wounds as best as you can. Try to forget what the other person is doing. You will find within yourself the resources to go on.

The temptation of suicide

You may be thinking of ending it all, wanting to feel no pain, wanting to disappear. You may be contemplating suicide. Believe me, this is not the answer.

There are two parts in a suicidal person; one wants to eliminate suffering by killing life, and the other wants to live. I urge you to go on living and to take care of your pain.

There are less radical and less destructive ways of buffering pain and suffering than taking one's own life.

Do not turn your inner rage on yourself. Express it outwardly. Hit a pillow, scream, make a drawing of your enemy and then tear it up and stomp on it.

If the desire to end your life becomes too strong, cry out for help, phone a friend, phone a hospital or a help line.

You may think that by committing suicide you will punish the person who left you. But if you really want to get back at the other person, show that you can become healed, vibrant and happy.

Contemplations

There is something worse that an unsatisfied desire, and that is a satisfied one. (Arabic)

I understand why Jesus asked us to forgive seventy-seven times seven. Every day, I forgive the one who hurt me.

The soul would not see rainbows if the eyes did not shed tears. (British)

Some take pleasure in going one better than anyone else in terms of pain and suffering. We should arrange a contest.

To the person who complained that since her loved one's death she has been feeling like an empty hour glass, I suggested that she turn the hour glass over.

Did you know that in the middle of the night, in the glow of the moon, there are waterfalls surrounded by rainbows.

If our hearts should condemn us, let us remember that God is greater than our hearts. (Saint John)

Chapter 5

I allow myself to heal

Healing

It is remembering having been loved,
without feeling the pang of that lost love.

It is breathing without the tension
of suppressed sobs.

It is no longer having a lump of sadness
in the throat.

It is coming out of the long incubation
of suffering.

It is being born to
a world unexpectedly beautiful.

It is being alone
without feeling isolated.

Accepting discomfort now to feel better soon

The sooner you accept your emotional hurt, the faster you will learn from it and be freed from it.

I have met a number of people who have waited much too long before being freed from their pain and turning to embrace life again. Here are some examples:

John, who did not know anything about the process of grieving, suffered from a 20-year depression after the death of his mother. One evening, while watching a drama he was so moved that he began to sob. This connected him to his deeply buried pain and triggered his process of grieving. By going through this he was finally able to let his mother go. He is no longer depressed.

A woman lost her nine-year old son during heart surgery. She was told by a psychic that her child was not dead and had already reincarnated. For years, she looked for him in all the newborn babies and children whom she met. All these years she neglected her family and nearly went crazy. She finally accepted the death of her child and the fact that she would see him again in his new resurrected body.

I met parents who, for 10 years, never talked about their child, who had died in its crib. When they were finally able to talk about the pain of that loss, they were able to accept the death of their child. They were liberated from their guilt and from mutual guilt-slinging. They could, once again, begin nurturing the love they had for one another.

I am sure that you do not want to wait that long to grieve and risk wasting years of your life. How long will you hide your discomfort, deny your pain and live in depression?

I assure you that you will survive this loss, and you will go on living to the fullest.

Embrace yourself

Welcome yourself with at least as much compassion as you would a sick friend.

Embrace yourself.

Accept the fact that for a while you are not as efficient as usual. You may feel upset and even shattered by this loss.

Like a convalescent, take it slowly, avoid difficult situations, put off making important decisions, stay away from emotionally needy people.

This feeling is temporary. You will soon be back to normal.

Most of all, do not blame yourself. The past is behind you. You have done what you felt was best for you. There are no mistakes, only events that can teach you how to live more fully.

I have made progress

I think that I am getting better.
I used to think about you every minute of the day
and I used to feel sad.

Now you come to mind every ten minutes or so
and it does not feel as painful.

One day soon I will not think of you for a whole hour,
for a whole day,
for a whole week.

Yet, I know that I will never forget you.

Letting go of the last hope

To let go of the last hope of getting your love back is not easy. It tugs at your heart, it haunts your soul, it feeds on the faintest hint of a possible reconciliation. But you cannot reactivate a dead volcano, make a desert bloom, revive a withered plant.

These efforts to patch up the relationship are often useless and painful. They can delay your healing process considerably.

Some say that maintaining a friendship with the one you once loved is possible. Perhaps. But three conditions must be met: you must be over the love relationship, you must have forgiven yourself, you must have forgiven the other person. Trying to befriend the one you have left or who has left you, immediately after the separation, is premature. In fact, it can prevent you from breaking the patterns of the love relationship.

Invest your energy in the healing process, make new friends, rediscover old friends, make new plans.

At times, you will have the urge to contact the person from whom you are separating. Welcome this urge without giving in to it. Remember your previous efforts to obtain the inaccessible. Ask a friend to help you.

A sage once observed: "Life does not repeat itself."

Caution: Do not rush your healing process

You are feeling better. You enjoy this new state. You are tempted to extend yourself in activities and gatherings that may be beyond your strength right now.

If you are the one who was left, you may want to engage in romantic affairs. You want to rebuild your self-image, you want to prove to yourself that you are still desirable and attractive. Maybe you just want to spread a balm on your wound.

Know that you are still vulnerable, and that affairs at this point may depress you more than help you. You may also be setting yourself up for another disappointment.

Save your energy.

Attend to your daily tasks.

Be fully aware of the healing process going on within you.

The best tonic remains the respectful friendship and support of a few loyal friends.

You are still lovable and desirable. Know that you will love again. Trust in the knowledge and truth of these words.

Not only you, but also my dreams

The more I let you go,
the more I peel you off like dead skin,
the more I let the memory of you fade away,
the more I realize it is not so much you that
I am giving up,
but my dreams.

Like an architect rolling up his plans,
like a set designer packing up her decor,
like a merchant putting away his display,
I, too, must gather up my dreams of love:
to live in the same house,
to work together,
to see the fruits of love ripen,
to grow old at your side.

You can go.
But what will I do
with my leftover dreams
after this painful realization?

There they lie like tangled piles of film
unravelled from the reel.

For you who believe in prayer

When you lose someone you love, prayer can bring you comfort. Knowing that there is a God of love can be very consoling.

Make sure that your prayer is not an excuse to hold on to the person who is gone.

> *"I talk to him everyday."*
> *"He is not gone, he is still with us."*

It is preferable to talk directly to God about how you feel.

If spontaneous prayer does not come to you, recite prayers that you know. The psalms in the Bible, for instance, can describe very well your emotional state.

True hope will not take root as long as the other person is still there in your imagination.

Once you have bid the other person goodbye, hope will fill you with a new presence. I will talk more about this later on.

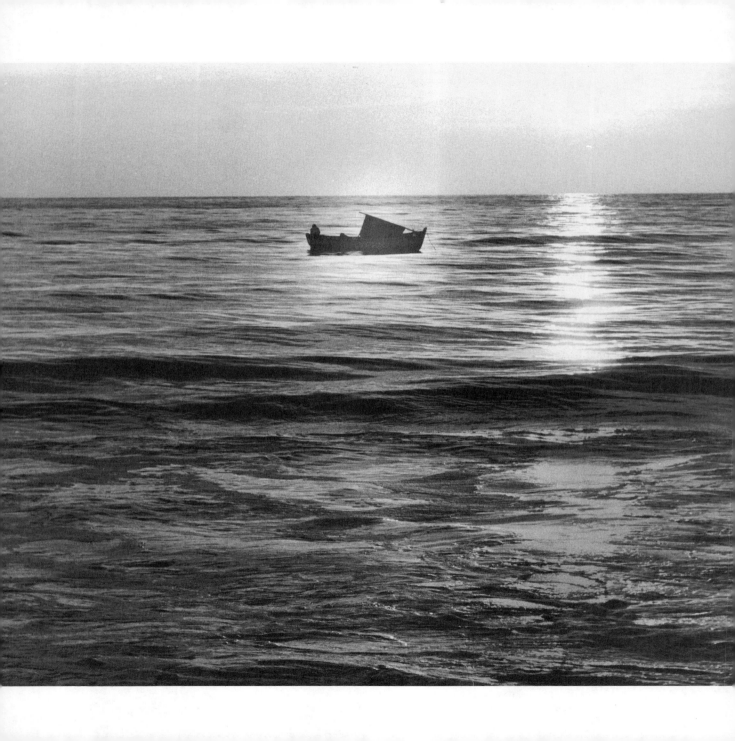

My boat is drifting

My boat was quietly floating on calm seas.
I was headed towards a safe and welcoming harbour.
Then suddenly the winds began to blow.
The sail started snapping frantically, my course was
altered.

Now the mast looks bare and useless.
The stays are on the verge of collapse.
The hull is inclining dangerously.
I have lost control, I nearly capsized.

I am no longer the captain of my ship.
My sighting is off.
My boat drifts rudderless, listing,
without horizon.
Hopeless, I hang on to the helm.

But once I have survived my initial panic,
once I have harnessed this gale,
that same wind which tried to throw me overboard now
fills my sail and propels me towards another peaceful harbour.

Prayer to a silent God

Sometimes God, I get angry with you,
with the suffering that my soul feels and that
my body refuses.

Sometimes, I ask you:
What do you mean by this loss?
What truth do you want to teach me?
What direction do you want me to take?

I know that you want to reveal something to me.
Sometimes, I get impatient with you and I feel that
you are taking too long to reveal your plan to me.

What to do with your memories

Memories keep the soul of the departed person attached to you, as it were.

At first, her things, her letters, the photographs, can help you survive. They recall the presence of the one who is absent.

After a while, you may realize that these mementos revive in you a painful presence. The person is there without being there.

As soon as you feel strong enough, if you want to encourage your grieving process, put the photos in an album or in a drawer, and give away the objects that belonged to your beloved.

To ease your separation from these things, you may want to keep one or two objects; perhaps a small photograph or some letters. These objects will help you make the transition.

Classified ad

Willing to sell or exchange for something of equal value.
The new moons and the full moons.
The Friday evenings and the Sunday afternoons.
The music we shared.
The fall scenery.

The colour of his hair.
The summer picnics.
The long talks.
The sound of his footsteps on the stairs.

The ring of his phone call in the evening.
To anyone interested, willing to let go many
other memories. Will consider any reasonable
offer.

Reason: personal.

Give yourself the right to go through it

For a while yet, you may feel depressed.

Refusing to play the role of the enthusiastic and energetic person is OK.

Protecting yourself is OK.

Crying may give you a feeling of relaxation, even purification.

Little by little you are opening up more deeply to a new world of emotions. By their very nature emotions move, change and evolve.

Try not to dwell on one particular feeling (sadness, anger, depression, and the like). Try to be still for a while and focus your attention on your inner turmoil until it has subsided.

Allow the dance of emotions to go on within you. Experience it and then let it subside. Life renews itself constantly.

Intermittent suffering

You can expect to experience emotional ups and downs for some time to come.

You may have quiet moments when you can forget by keeping busy. You may even feel that your grief is coming to an end. Then when you least expect it, anxiety and pain will surface and the dance of sad memories will start again!

A weekend, a holiday, an anniversary, a scene, a significant place, an event or a piece of music may bring you right back to the feeling of grief. If you feel strong enough, you should try to go into this painful and dark corner of your soul and attempt to understand its source. If not, try not to be overwhelmed by it. It may be better for now to avoid those painful feelings by finding a distraction.

You have the right to get angry

During this period of grief, you have the right to let your anger rise and express itself, in spite of all the social taboos forcing you to repress it. Know that this feeling of anger is different from hatred or resentment. Anger, once expressed, will disappear. Resentment, if cultivated, will keep emerging and gnawing away at your heart.

Let your anger rise. Tell your lost love that you are angry with her for having left you, for having abandoned you, for having forced you to take over the responsibilities that she used to handle, for forcing you to mature too rapidly.

Feel free to be angry with social conventions, fate, God, those who hinder your grieving process, those who abandon you.

Be grateful that you can feel and express this anger. Some people who experience tragedies repress their anger and turn it on themselves. They end up feeling guilty and depressed to the point of developing physical and psychological ailments.

To remain sane, you must accept your feelings of anger and find healthy outlets for it, such as exercising, beating a pillow or a mattress, screaming in your car or in the woods, and so on.

The dance of emotions

Black depression is swirling around my soul.
Yellow fear is stomping its heavy feet.
Red anger restrains my movements, growling.
Greenish love tiptoes around.

Blue sorrow is worried about disrupting this round, if it
breaks out.
Like shadows, my emotions appear and disappear against
a grey backdrop.

Remember that you are still fragile

Some days you may feel drained and unmotivated. Be sure not to burden yourself with "should's" and "should not's." Remember that you are still vulnerable.

There is no need to try to play the hero, to make important decisions or to get involved in pointless romantic affairs.

Take care of your health; get lots of rest, eat well and exercise.

Avoid pushy salespeople,
needy people and
stressful situations.

Fight the tendency to be idle by doing simple exercises (walking, biking ...).

Do not forget your wise and faithful friend, Mother Nature. Give yourself time to commune with fresh air, water, trees and skies.

Suffering has made you more alive

Suffering has forced you out of your complacency,
out of your inner, middle-class comfort.
You were stuffed, satiated, full of torpor.
Your loss has caused you a rude awakening.
Your present neediness helps you appreciate
the small joys of life.

You may have noticed how easy it is to find pleasure with
things and people that you never really noticed before:
the colour of the leaves, a greeting from the mailman,
a simple handshake, a colleague's smile,
the sound of certain footsteps,
the intensity of a child's game,
ice glistening in the sun, clouds drifting across a blue sky,
a summer rainfall,
spontaneous prayers,
love songs with their happy, and sad, endings.

Suffering can sharpen your senses,
open your heart,
help you see life in a new light.

"Blessed are the pure (or purified) in spirit
for they will inherit the earth."

I have sensitive skin

Because of the void caused by your absence,
I have been afraid of being unable to love again,
to share myself again,
to trust again.

My scars are still fresh.
I am afraid to touch them.
The skin is still so thin.
I am suspicious.

I want to be consoled,
but I do not want to be approached.
I want to be understood
but I do not want to reveal myself.

I am not ready to trust.
I want to give,
but I am afraid of being rejected
if I take the first step.
Please understand me!

When sadness has a hold on you

Surely you are familiar with the social myth that sadness, distress and destruction are proof that your love is real.

Dying of sorrow because of the loss of love, or of the beloved, would demonstrate a deep attachment, whereas to go on living and be happy would indicate a superficial, even hypocritical, love.

Such a belief is unfounded. Someone who develops a devotion to sadness is more influenced by social pressures than by his or her inner life.

Be wary of self-pity that can be used to elicit the compassion of others. To ask openly for their sympathy and friendship is easier, and certainly more effective.

There is a certain beauty in sorrow as long as it is short lived and life-giving.

When will you love again?

Just a short while ago you were declaring that you would never love again. You were giving up on love and perhaps you believed that God had created it to torture human hearts.

However, if you are still reading this book, you are probably willing to go through the grieving process, to heal and to live fully again. You may still be hesitant in believing in love. This hesitation comes less from the fear of love than from the fear of suffering.

The day will come when you have regained your self-confidence and your trust in life. Then you will also know whom, and how, you will love.

You will then accept being in love, while knowing that you will also suffer, in one way or another.

Being true to your love

As we know now, being faithful to your love does not mean dying or destroying yourself.

If you really want to be true to someone you have loved, and keep alive her memory, put yourself in her presence mentally and ask her what she expects of you. Let her respond.

"
. . . .
. . . .
. . . .
. . . . "

This inner dialogue will give you clear directions for your life.

Your beloved will tell you to honour her by living fully, growing and loving again.

You carry within you the wisdom, and the legacy, of a deep and emotional bond between you and your beloved.

Give yourself permission to heal at your own pace

You will find that very few people around you can tolerate your suffering. They will want you to feel better, to forget, to accept, to distract yourself.

They will try to prevent you from hurting. Yet, you must understand that you have every right to go through this painful experience.

Consequently you should avoid hiding your feelings behind a composed front, a pretend smile, a false attitude.

Avoid mixing with people who have denied their own pain, or who display the physical and mental signs of repressed grief.

Regardless of the theories on the stages, and the duration, of the grieving process, remember that your experience is unique. Here performance and speed are not required. You have the right to deal with your grief in your own way and at your own pace.

I am on the right track

I spend less time on inner questioning.
I feel less vulnerable.
I am able to enjoy beautiful scenery.

My thoughts are clearer.
My judgement is more acute.
My feelings are more stable.

I get satisfaction from my work.
I see life in a whole new way.
I recognize expressions on people's faces that I could not see before.

I take pleasure in the small joys of daily life.
I feel like sharing my new-found enthusiasm.
I sense a new life sprouting within me.

Must you be born to death as you are to life?

In Ingmar Bergman's movie "Cries and Whispers," a woman in agony prolongs her dying. She wants to be loved before she embraces her fate. Her two sisters are unable to give her the comfort she needs.

She cannot die before love gives meaning to her death. Then a young maid, a peasant, takes her in her arms and places her head on her naked breasts. This expression of love and compassion allows the old woman to move on to the next life.

All of you who have left someone, or who have been left, without a message of love, may need to seek a sign of affection that will help you surrender to your emotions.

To all of you who may feel that way, I extend a gesture of friendship that will allow you to deal with your grief and be born to new life.

Someone loves you

To the man or the woman who has lost a spouse without exchanging a message of love.

To the couple who is torn apart by quarrelling.

To the parent who has lost a child in an accident.

To the person forced to retire.

To the woman whose dreams of motherhood are disappearing.

To the middle-aged man realizing that he abandoned his adolescent dreams.

To the married couple who has recently separated.

To the unemployed.

To the child who is moved from one foster home to another.

To those of you who have lost a loved one without saying goodbye.

To the abandoned lover.

To the youth leaving home for the first time.

To the single mother separated from her child.
To the aging woman whose strength is abandoning her.
To the child going off to school for the first time.

To you who are right now grieving your own private sorrow.

If those you have left behind are unable to tell you how much they appreciate you, I will tell you: "You are great, you have loved and you have fulfilled your commitment to the best of your ability, you are important."

I love you.

Chapter 6

 I am growing

Growing

Being attached to you
has revealed to me my selfishness
and my selflessness,
has brought me in touch with my tenderness
and my harshness,
has helped me discover my sensuality
and my spirituality,
has helped me recognize the child within
and the adult in me.

Becoming detached from you
has allowed me to get in touch with my sadness
and my joy,
has taken me to the depth of despair
and freedom,
has helped me find myself dependent
and courageous,
has revealed to me my fear of death
and my inner resources.

When all is said and done,
I have no regrets.

Because you have loved you are not the same

You are not the same person that you were before this experience of love.

Love and suffering have opened gateways to new worlds.

You are more sensitive and less afraid of pain.
You are more committed but less dependent.
You have learned to invest yourself
without losing yourself.

You are more self-assured.
You are ready to love again.

I was carrying an unknown treasure

With shame, I dragged around my sack of sorrow.
I sought relief and comfort from everyone around me.
They all avoided the miserable beggar that I had become.
(There are happy beggars who attract people.)

Then I met an angel, on my journey, who taught me to
open my bag and to look through it very carefully.
I discovered, in the folds of my sack, my desire for the
Divine.
I began to glimpse the abundance of my
inner wealth.
Now, with joy, I swing my sack of
dreams.

Can betrayal help you grow?

I am not sure I should ask you this question. But I have. If the person you love has not met your expectations; if your loved one has deprived you of a right, or worse, abandoned you, you may feel let down, offended, betrayed. Something is broken within you, cut off between you and your beloved.

This feeling is very common in families where the children's development causes inevitable emotional ruptures; parents feel betrayed and children feel betrayed.
> *"After all I have done for him."*
> *"My parents do not understand me."*
> *"Children are ungrateful."*
> *"My parents will not let me grow up."*

It may take a while before you understand how these feelings of betrayal help you to grow. Like the baby bird with feeble wings, you felt tossed out of the nest by the very person that you most trusted. Hopefully, you will come to appreciate the lessons this experience has taught you.

Just as the ropes that hold a hot air balloon must be untied for it to rise, abandonment may urge you abruptly onward to self-fulfilment.

How to deal with holidays and special days

A friend who accompanies families through their grieving process recommends that they always prepare themselves for a coming holiday or anniversary. He suggests that the family gather for a grieving session shortly beforehand.

The members of the family may look at photographs, recall memorable events, exchange thoughts, allow themselves to mourn and to be consoled. After this session, they are able to celebrate the event joyfully, without guilt.

Even for those of you who are further along in your grieving, anniversaries, birthdays and other memorable events may cause you sadness for a few hours, or a day. You should embrace this partial relapse into grief and experience it fully. You will then be able to celebrate the event more intensely.

From isolation to solitude

Will the pain of separation lead you to isolation or to solitude?

If you have a tendency to close yourself off, you should ask yourself whether you are becoming comfortable with solitude or simply isolating yourself.

Isolation can resemble solitude, but there is a great difference between these two inner attitudes. You may be experiencing both at the same time, or in turn.

Here are some pointers to help you determine whether you are experiencing barren isolation or life-giving solitude.

Isolation is

the fear of being with others
and the fear of being alone,

a defense system against
intrusion,

inner turmoil and confusion,

a distressed outlook,

a closing to the outer world,

a continuous and useless series
of speculations,

the denial of your own vulner-
ability caused by fear of
rejection,

a time of inner and outer unrest.

Solitude is

a voluntary withdrawal from others
to be alone with yourself,

an inner contemplation helping you to
be more open to yourself and to others,

an open and peaceful time of
reflecting on yourself,

a peaceful outlook,

an opening to others through intimacy
with yourself,

a silence filled with the love of those
around you,

the profound acceptance of your own
interdependence and your own
autonomy,

a time of peace and of harmonizing
your inner world.

From the desert to the inner oasis

You may have to experience isolation before you reach a comfortable and life-giving state of solitude. Each one of us reacts differently to the idea of being alone. Some of us collapse and regress, others will rebel against any form of dependence.

As a child you may have felt afraid of being abandoned or rejected. Consequently, you may feel that loneliness is a terrible threat. If so, your initial reaction will be to deny your reality or to distract yourself with television, music, love affairs, alcohol, drugs, and the like. Finding a guide or a counsellor who can help you understand solitude as something good and life-giving is important.

On this journey to inner discovery, you will learn to go from isolation to solitude, from loneliness to aloneness. It will be as though you were finding a cure in the disease itself, or discovering that you have to push the hook deeper into the flesh to remove it.

Stay with yourself.
Discover all of your parts.
Plunge all the way into your inner spring.

Armed with courage, you will walk through the ruins of your own suffering, through the dark and damp caves of your inner world. You will pass through many chambers and your faith will lead you to the heart of your essence where lies a precious jewel. Then you will know who you are and what you are called to do.

"I am never alone with my solitude."

Who invented the word failure?

Life is not a match. It does not end with a loss, and never results in failure.

But like a fighter who has been dealt a blow, you must pick yourself up to avoid being hit again.

You will come out a winner if you learn from this experience. Take stock of the lessons that you have learned:

You know yourself better.
You understand the suffering of others better.
You are freer.
You have opened up your horizons.
You know that you are not perfect.
You allow others to be imperfect.
You are on the road to healing.

You are like a scientist who makes a ground-breaking discovery with a wrong formula.

You are like a painter who creates a masterpiece from a stain on the canvas.

You are like a musician who writes a symphony from a faulty chord.

There are no mistakes or failures; life always rises from death.

An inner smile

Within me a smile is rising,
vibrating,
expanding,
in the silence of my heart.

It lightens my being,
and brightens my life.

Because I have loved,
I want to love again.

It is time to change

Now that you feel better,
that you can concentrate again,
that the future is open to you,
that the past is a memory, it is time to change.

You are no longer a prisoner of your old relationship.
Make all the necessary adjustments in your life.
You have more time to meet your own needs.
Develop new interests.
Change your style of dress.

Try something new, something exhilarating.
Travel to new places.
Go back to school.
Make new friends.
Join a new club.
Remodel your home.
Learn something you have always wanted to know, or master.

I have seen my own sadness in your eyes

My heart was ripe with bitterness,
my gaping wound filled with venomous thoughts.
I could scarcely contain my wrath.

To forgive, to try to forget, was like betraying myself.
I needed vengeance, retribution, or else I would feel forever
humiliated.
To meet the person who hurt me seemed like sheer folly.

But when I finally mustered the courage
to look upon her face, her expression moved me to the core of
my being.
In her eyes, I recognized my own sadness, my depression,
a hint of tenderness.

Since that moment, that vision haunts me.
All those feelings were shared by her and me.
My heart was touched, it softened and opened up.
All the harshness vanished.
Compassion had its way.

I am proud of myself

When my hurt was still fresh,
I wanted to make you feel guilty,
like a child who hits a smaller child, when he is hurt.

I wanted you to be overwhelmed by remorse at the thought
of the pain that you inflicted on me.
I wanted to place you on the stand, to let the entire world
know about your betrayal.
I wanted to punish you, to take my revenge.
I wanted to come out triumphant, remorseless.

I am proud of myself for having avoided this treacherous
road.
Many times I have felt anger, but I have not given into it by
punishing you.
Though I felt like avenging myself, I understood how
useless it would be.

I am proud of myself for having embraced my hurt.
I tended to it with all the care I could muster.
I have chosen to protect what I have loved.
Through it all, I have grown.

Forgiving myself

I want to forgive myself for having been
fragile,
careless,
wrong,
vulnerable in love,
unsuspecting,
hurt,
a dreamer,
frustrated and lonely,
willing to love again.

In short,
I want to forgive myself
for being "human."

Forgiving the other person

Granting forgiveness is a royal gesture.
As soon as you feel strong enough, forgive the other person.

Forgiving does not mean forgetting the offense or the
separation,
    making excuses for the other person,
    denying your emotions or your feelings,
    reconciling yourself with the other person.

Forgiving means freeing yourself from vengeance and
resentment,
    recognizing that the other person can learn from the pain
that he has caused,
    recognizing the joy of being forgiven by others,
    asking for the strength to love beyond this wounded love,
    relieving the other person of his debt and wishing him well.

If you can forgive, you too will become a queen, a king.

Forgive him, forgive her

Forgive him, forgive her
for leaving,
for leaving so soon,
for leaving without saying goodbye,
for leaving without preparing you,
for leaving without fulfilling all the promises,
for leaving with a piece of yourself,
for leaving with your world of dreams and aspirations.

Trusting yourself to trust others

This separation from your beloved greatly undermined your self-confidence and your trust in others.

Initially you felt that you had to prove to yourself that you were lovable and capable of loving again.

Now you know that you are lovable. You only have to welcome those people that Providence will place on your path.

Go out, meet people.
Rediscover your neighbours, your colleagues.
Join a group, a community of friends.
Invite people for coffee.
Share information, services.
Listen to people; they love talking about themselves.

You can now face the inevitable losses of your life

You are now master of a new skill – the art of letting go of people, activities and things that come in and out of your life.

There are people who carry around the sorrows of all their unresolved losses; they are like cluttered trunks. They never let go of their mother, their father, their first teddy bear, their cat, their childhood, their childhood friends, and so on.

By fully experiencing the grief of this separation from your beloved, all at once, you have gotten rid of everything that was dead inside you.

The next time you are faced with the loss of someone important, you will still experience shock, pain and turmoil, but you will know your way on the road to healing.

You have succeeded this time around, you will succeed again.

By learning how to live after death, little by little you are learning how to die after life. The inevitability of your own death will no longer be as frightening.

By overcoming small deaths you will discover different perspectives on living.

Growing a garden in foreign ground

Like a seed thrown in the spring wind,
my love and my hope are carried by the breath
of your presence.

Like a bountiful Mother Nature, carefree, drunk with joy,
I am planting my garden in foreign ground.
With every thrust of germination, with each sprout,
I am realizing the richness of my treasure.

In these moments of joy, ecstasy and discovery,
I bask in this abundance of life.
I marvel, I rejoice, I aspire to
be the proud new owner,
the undisputed landlord of these grounds.

Who would have guessed that I had sown my dreams
on someone else's property.
Then one day my host brings me back to reality.

I have become the usurper in an occupied territory.
I am asked to leave this rich soil.

My fruits and my flowers are growing on foreign ground.
I want to leave without turning back.
I want to hide my pain behind a mask, hardened by pride.
I want to forget all my days of cultivating and
uproot the fruit of my labour like an unwanted growth.

Then, with the humility of a king turned beggar,
I begin picking, plucking, reaping and gathering my inner
harvest.
I must dig, cut and even pull out the roots, to take
everything.
I refuse to leave anything to my spiteful host.

Reaping what you have sown during the relationship

You are beginning to feel less and less of the pain of your separation. You can go for long periods without even thinking about the loss of your beloved.

The time has come for you to reap the fruits of your relationship.

Take up new interests.

Learn a new sport.

Learn a new skill.

Try a new approach to life.

Discover a new you.

Make a list of the attributes that you liked in the other person. Note that these qualities that you were looking for in the other person, you also possess within yourself. Now, these belong to you:

kindness,

assertiveness,

love of music, of literature,

self-care,

social values, and the like.

Do not let your beloved go without claiming your legacy. It is up to you to self-actualize what you have loved, sought and admired in the other person.

Janet takes back what belongs to her

Janet is a single secretary who fell head over heels in love with her boss, Jim. He is married with three children. Their initial friendship soon turned into an intense love affair.

When Janet came to see me, she was devastated by this impossible situation. She was increasingly depressed. Her mental health was affected and she felt terrible, guilty about Jim's wife.

After hesitating for weeks, she decided to end the relationship. I helped her prepare to meet with Jim and formally end the relationship. After she had done this, Janet came back to see me. She was weeping and overwhelmed by sadness. I supported her during her time of grief. After a period of about nine months, I suggested that, when she felt ready, she should think of claiming her legacy.

Two weeks later, Janet arrived at my office, still hurting, but feeling more peaceful. She felt ready for the ritual of claiming her legacy. She sat in front of an empty chair and tried to imagine that Jim was sitting in front of her. She began describing the qualities that attracted her to him – his compassion, his sense of humour, his generosity, his public speaking abilities and his sensuality.

I asked her to focus on these qualities and to draw a symbol representing each one. She drew an ear, a happy face, a mouth and open hands.

Then she proceeded to tell Jim to give her back the compassion that she had loaned him and that he had made his own. She stood up and placed the drawing of the ear on her heart and sat down again.

Next, I calmly invited her to reclaim this compassion and to make room for it inside her. Judging by how her face lit up and how her body relaxed, I knew that the process was having positive results. Her claiming of the other qualities had the same beneficial effects. She left my office looking radiant and feeling energized.

During the following week, Jim broke his promise never to be alone with her. He invited her to meet him privately. Janet was shaken by Jim's insistence, but was able to tell him that though she still loved him, it was now different. She did not need him in the same way. She gave him a hug and left.

Taking possession of your legacy

I want to introduce you to a wonderful ritual which will help you reclaim what you have lost. I suggest that you perform this exercise in the company of a few close friends. This will help you bring the process to completion. If you do it alone, you may experience reservations and hesitations, and give up halfway. I assure you that the act of claiming your legacy will bring about a profound and liberating transformation within yourself.

Ask one of your friends to guide you through the following steps.

1. Imagine that the person you lost is sitting in front of you (use an empty chair to symbolize the person).

2. Describe what you liked in the person: qualities, strengths, attributes.

3. Represent each one of these by a drawing or an object and place them on the chair in front of you.

4. Out loud, say the following: "I take back (name a quality) that I loaned you, as well as all the maturity and growth that your personality added to it." You are now harvesting the fruits of your love. (See the poem, "Growing a garden in foreign ground," on page 149.)

5. Stand up, take the drawing or the symbol and place it on your heart. Allow yourself to feel physically touched by this newly discovered quality. The incubation period may last over 20 minutes. During this period, your friend can help you try out this new quality, feel it deeply and act it out in different contexts.

6. Do the same thing for each quality.

7. When you are finished, find a symbol that best describes your lover's personality and place the drawings and objects around that symbol to form a complete picture.

8. Your guide proclaims to the group that you have completed your process of grieving.

You will be amazed at the transformation that will take place within you during the next few days.

The fruits of your loss

Suffering is meaningless without claiming your legacy.

Your departure revealed
my needs,
my expectations,
my shortcomings,
my dependence.
I did not think I could live without you.

Now that you are gone,
I feel alone and complete at the same time.
I have learned to like the music you loved.
I find myself admiring that which you admired.
I have discovered your areas of interest.
I have started to cook.
I now paint.

I realized that I could help myself, care for myself,
support myself.
I no longer need you to make me feel important.
I am no longer your better half, I am whole.

The strengths I admired in you,
I found them in myself.
They were there, in need of nourishment
and of room to grow.

In your absence, a miracle is occurring inside me.
The valleys of my soul are being filled,
the river beds flow with gushing waters.

I am discovering new sources of energy.
I am enriched by my love for you.

After reconciling with yourself, will you be able to reconcile with the other person?

Reconciling with yourself is the most important step. Reconciling with the other person is a sign of complete recovery.

John and Helen are separated but still appreciate getting together to talk about their children.

Paul and Louise spend an evening together occasionally to discuss the many things they still have in common.

Jack always consults his ex-wife on matters regarding his budget.

I feel that a reconciliation is possible if three conditions are met.

1. You must be completely detached emotionally from the other person, otherwise there is a risk of falling back into the old patterns of the relationship.

2. Both of you must have healed your own wounds.

3. Both of you must have matured and become emotionally autonomous.

Very few couples can transform a once hurtful relationship into a fruitful friendship.

You will be filled with a new presence

If you are still looking for the one you lost in your life, if you want to see her again, if you are saddened by the mere thought of him, you have not yet let go completely.

If your grieving process is not over yet, be certain that one day you will be filled with a new and life-giving presence. You will recognize it by the joy, the peace and the freedom it gives you.

This awakening often feels like giving birth for women. Men feel like an enormous weight has been lifted from their shoulders.

Your memory will recall the presence of the one you lost; but your love for this person will give this presence new life.

You will no longer be consumed with just physical longing, but by the love you felt for that person. The beloved will no longer be outside of you but living within you in a spiritual way.

All the energy of your love will return to you when you let your beloved go completely.

A young woman to her deceased husband

You are gone now!
Even though you promised, with or without words,
that you would always love me,
that you would always be by my side,
that you would always be there when I needed you,
that you would always share my joys and my sorrows.

You are gone now!
And though I revealed myself to you,
there are still so many things that I wanted to say,
so many feelings that I wanted to express,
so many plans that I wanted to fulfil.

You are gone now!
Gradually, I let you go,
I forgive you for leaving so soon, I forget our dreams,
I recover my energy, I ask you to forgive me.

You are gone now!
I know that some day I will stop dying with you,
that the memory of you will be as light and as fragile
as a smile, that a new presence will fill me up,
that all that I loved in you will live inside me.
Then I will be reborn through you.

A mother's breakthrough

During a group session, a woman who had lost a baby was able to say goodbye to her child.

A week later, she woke up in the night and experienced an important transformation. She felt very comfortable compared to the many times that she had waken up at night, filled with anxiety.

Here is what she described:

"I could see pins piercing my heart but I felt no pain.
I understood that I had forgiven myself.
I was able to pray that night.
I was filled with the presence of God, like on the day of my first communion.

This experience enriched me.
I felt beautiful.
Like someone giving birth.
I felt forever transformed."

Congratulations!

You have survived.
You have learned how to go on living.
You know how to love.

You know how to let go.
You know how to heal.
You know how to grow.

You know how to live.

I never thought I could thank you and congratulate myself

Because I have known you, I am not the same.

Thank you for
the love,
the care,
the support,
the gifts,
the romantic dinners,
the exchanges,
the hopes,
the plans,
your intelligence.

Thank you for the separation,
for the opportunity to grow.
I congratulate myself for
questioning my life,
reflecting on myself,
examining my way of loving,

discovering my inner strengths,
exploring the value of suffering,
making new friends and rediscovering old ones,
becoming more sensitive,
expanding my capacity to love,
completing my grieving process.

About the author

Jean Monbourquette is a priest, psychologist and professor at Saint Paul University, Ottawa, where he acts as trainer and supervisor in Family and Community Group Work at the University's Pastoral Institute.

He has a licentiate in theology and Master's degrees in philosophy and education from the University of Ottawa, a Master's degree in clinical psychology from the University of San Francisco and a doctorate in transformational psychology from the International College of Los Angeles. His thesis investigated masculine spirituality from a Jungian perspective. His clinical approach is based on neuro-linguistic programming.

He has done research on the relationship between psychology and spirituality, especially in terms of the grieving process, ways to support the dying, the psycho-spiritual process of forgiveness and masculine violence.

He is the author of numerous books and magazine articles including *Aimer, perdre et grandir,* the original French version of *To Love Again,* which has sold 80,000 copies. He also presents lectures and workshops in Canada, Europe and South America.

imprimerie   gagné ltêe

PRINTED IN CANADA